Somebody Like You

Also by T. Carmi

THE BRASS SERPENT

T. Carmi

Somebody Like You

Poems translated from the Hebrew by
Stephen Mitchell

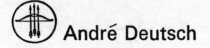 André Deutsch

First published 1971 by
André Deutsch Limited
105 Great Russell Street, London WC1

Copyright © 1971 by T. Carmi
Translation in this edition © Stephen Mitchell

Printed in Great Britain by
Clarke, Doble and Brendon Ltd
Plymouth

ISBN 0 233 95961 0: hardback edition
ISBN 0 233 95963 7: paperback edition

Contents

Acknowledgments

'A View of Jerusalem' has appeared in *Midstream*; 'Transition' in *The Humanist*; 'The Unicorn Looks in the Mirror', 'The Sacrifice', 'Night of Mirrors' and 'Examination of Conscience Before Going to Sleep' in *Poetry Review*; 'Condition' in *The Journals of Pierre Menard*; 'In Memory of Leah Goldberg' in *European Judaism*; 'Four Air Letters' in *The Times Literary Supplement*; 'To the Pomegranate Tree', 'The Stranger', 'Landscapes', 'Somebody Like You', 'Song of Friendship', 'Girl in the Closet', 'Shockwaves' and 'Memorial Day, 1969' in *Modern Poetry in Translation*; 'Still Life' in *Adam International Review*.

Translator's Note

Most of the poems in this selection come from Mr Carmi's latest books: *The Unicorn Looks in the Mirror* (1967) and *Collected Poems* (1970). They are not in chronological order.

I am grateful to Mr Carmi for his encouragement and for the care with which he read and criticized my translations.

S.M.

The Unicorn Looks in the Mirror

Madam,
had you not held this mirror
to my face,

I would never have known
that I am melancholy, that my neck
is proud, that only one horn
grows from my forehead, and my beard
is wispy, and my lips too thick.

Madam,
let there be no anger,
no reproach – for had your bitter hand
not held this mirror
to my face,

I would never have dared
to approach, to rest
my cloven hooves
on your lap.

Madam,
had you not summoned my body's
echo, we would never
have become three:
I, and you, and my self,
and above us
a horn,
lengthening.

The Stranger

Opposite the painting
the stranger passes his finger
over the frame, and his eyes
bite into the indifferent apple.

The stranger, on the banks of the rug,
stops, extends
a hesitating foot. He sits down
slowly, and the chair
asks him many questions
behind his back.

Afterwards, he looks through the window
and recognizes a bare tree,
waiting in the cold, on a mountain ridge,
and one bird.

*

The trouble is,
he must hurry from place to place.
The trouble is, on the next day
he will see tooth-marks in the flesh of the apple,
the rug rising to greet him, the armchair
rubbing against his leg like a cat.
The stranger needs to uproot himself from here,
tomorrow, in order to plant
another bird in his eyes.

*

Will you come to me today, tonight?
And if you come – who are you?

But, at this moment,
as I stand opposite the window-frame,
I have the right to ask.

Landscapes

1
A white bird over a green river; two;
then three.
One telegraph-pole; two;
three bushes.
More than that (roofs,
clouds, blades of grass)
is hard to count from a train,
so I won't mention them.
In fact, I think I'll note
just one bird.
Maybe just its wings.

2
He was standing at the top of a tree,
dressed in blue overalls,
sawing.

      Suddenly
his face gaped,
his body twisted like a branch,
his hands filled with wind,
and he fell.

All this I saw
from the window of a train,
after a green meadow
and before a team of horses.
I note only the fact
of his falling.
I didn't hear
the scream.

Song of Friendship

My friend, my brother, dearest of all my friends,
For whom I would walk through fire and the many waters.
And one day I felt the army of his eyes
On the back of my neck; he said: 'I wish you were

Dead.' Oh angels scurried up and down;
A cow – naked! – hiccuped on the roof;
Pomegranates split like thunder; vines
Shed their skins; an ocean froze like ashes.

My friend, my brother, understood my mind;
To him the chambers of my heart were opened
Wide; he came, went, planted dreams in me;
He asked, solved; committed me to death.

Since then I'm very careful: in the kitchen,
In the pool, and at major intersections.

Songs without a Name

When you give a child the name of a bird – it loses the bird.

JOYCE CARY

I'm only saying these things,
because they began and ended a long time ago;
if I didn't know what their end was,
I would be able to write them as poems.

1

All night I couldn't sleep: I was biting your name in the pillow, and your name wept till dawn. All night the hangers in the closet made music, like triangles in a children's orchestra.

2

I'm choking you with my body. Only one thing can justify this abomination: that you are the air I breathe.

3

My hands are quiet like the window of your room, filled with clouds and air: my eyes are opened wide: the thing, and not its opposite.

4

It was only yesterday that you told me your name, and already it is swarming within me like schoolboys at recess. Only yesterday – and already it is swooping within me, like gulls toward the floating bread.

5

All these people in the streets, all these masks – do they love? I must put on a mask. Otherwise my face will be lost in the yards and in the rivers.

6

A clear mirror before your face and your hand. I put my hand on your breast. I put my mother beside you. And my childhood rises within me, and falls asleep.

7

Your sleep builds no wall or city of refuge. You let me walk around in the shadow of your eyelashes. My head on your shoulder, and your palm open.

8

They laugh at us, and they're right. The lamp burns without candles, the floor flows without shores, the window is always open. We have forgotten what it means to close. We remember everything; we laugh, and we're right.

I'm only saying these things,
because they began and ended a long time ago;
if I hadn't seen what their end was,
I would have written them as poems.

9

I can still explain to all of you what a lie is. Like someone who has been there on a visit, for a short time, many years ago.

10

My thirty-five years. I will open them one by one, put you in each one of them like cinnamon into an antique spice-box. When the day comes, they will all understand that I carried your fragrance inside me. Against their will they will answer, Amen.

11

I walk in the street, spring within spring, and think the thoughts of the coming winter. My eyes are veiled with snow, my hands still warm.

12

The night-birds that you put inside me fly away at dawn.
But I know that wherever I shut my eyes they will return.
Like your hand to my head.

13

Our beginning still laughs; therefore let us count the ends:
once I saw a sudden bird hit a windowpane and break its
neck; once I watched a premature spring abandon its fruit to
the frost; once, on my flowing bed, drought gushed within
me.

14

On the birthday of her love, she dressed in black. From her
feet to her festive hair, her clothing was black. His hand
became bony, his eyes flamed. He understood, he touched
her, and all her black answered:

15

Not after my death, and not in twenty years, and not in a
week. Tomorrow – what will remain tomorrow? Oh, we are
changing into ancient things. Time flows over us, the clouds
polish our faces. We are being gathered.

I'm only saying these things,
because even then we began
to collect each other.

16

Your name tears open my eyes in the morning, and shuts
   them at night.
I do not say much.
You know.
Your name shuts my eyes to the morning, and tears them
   open to night.

17

This wind will stop and this flower will fade. This house
will collapse and this man will fall. This woman will sin and
my sin will die with her. We will remain, with words that
blossom for one night, that have no cycle, no season, no bed.

I wrap myself in you each morning. My lips move, my legs are dumb. There is no point in asking when I do not give. There is no point in begging when you do not refuse. There is no point in singing.

I'm only saying these things.
You cannot bless the new moon
when you stand still.

19

The street was empty. Strange children came and wrote your name. I erased everyone with a giant sponge.

20

The moment I pause, you begin to move toward me. The moment I stop in my flight, you blow at me from all sides. I mustn't linger.

21

My memory kneels and tenses like a runner. When the signal is given, I am wrenched from your night and from you. My heart drums. My lungs scream toward the finish-line.

22

Your name gets smaller and smaller in my terrified skies. I am transporting you to a land that has no borders, passports, customs-officers. I have no belongings to hide, nothing to declare. But that field – it is entirely mine. A heritage forever and oblivion.

23

Yes, I'm always ready to run away. All I need is a crevice, a slit like the pupil of a skinny cat's eye. If you shut your eyes for an instant, the darkness will be my door. And when I return, I will touch the doorposts of your face, and my hand will not come back clean.

24
In order to clean the windowpane, you must soil it.
In order to return, you must turn.
I turn to you and ask:
Where should I go now that the answer has been given
and I can no longer return?

25
Your name gets smaller and smaller. The air grows empty.
Already I cannot divide firmament from firmament.

I have only said these things,
because I knew what their end was.
Now I am ready again,
and wait for the sound of the wings of a large bird
that doesn't know a thing:
not the name of a season,
not the address of a nest,
not the direction of a wind.
I am waiting for the sound of the wings of a large bird
that doesn't know my name.

Those Who Go on Voyages

Those who go on voyages seldom come back holy.

1

Even before he set forth
he already had the face of a man
who must double back:

unshaven, one of his eyes
servile, the other one dodging
the camera's quick trap.

He filled out the forms in a hurry,
he was all ready to go,
had a date with a strange tongue:

cracked mounds in the garden,
a woman growing wild,
cobwebs of old words in the nursery.

Then he said to his friends:

O my friends, o my dear ones,
water and fix, spray and prune –
I'll be back soon.

2

Then he set forth:

He clambered up the ladder
which her high dream had placed,
he skipped up and called to her: follow me! –

and brandished his foot above her.

He descended and ascended and descended,
he bumped and he shoved and he thumped
all the angels he met.

Then he stopped on the way:

18

All at once he opened his years
like an antique spice-box,
and filled them with the strange fragrance.

Oh myrrh and mountains of frankincense,
we have a little sister; this
is the day, and what shall we do? !

We'll talk. And he went on his way.

He flew toward the naked light :
barren, barren – he cursed –
who bore me in wrath, still-born.

He slammed his eyes and said :
my love hasn't gone to eternity,
only to the next room.

Then he lingered on the way :

He sat in the street, pleading :
I have no defenses at all,
like a snail out of its shell;

entered the strange house,
flooded it with brightness,
then left – and forgot to switch it off.

He nested in the street, chirping :
O my soul – o cover my cage
with a black curtain, and I'll be quiet;

rested his head on her breast,
rested his head like a stone,
then left – and forgot to roll it off.

I'm only a broken statue :
the soles of my feet are waiting
for the wisdom of expert hands;

gave her his prowess as a present,
the smile of his youth as a tip,
then left – and forgot to leave it.

Then he set forth :

Near ones, good-bye, dear ones,
forget me not, sweetie, the photographer's
waiting for the other eye.

He opened both eyes and surrendered them :
drooled onto his image
and thirstily drank his face.

Then he set forth :

He declared everything, candidly :
so many dead angels
(the gift of my clumsy foot),

and a ladder (not mine) for sale;
so many bags of second-hand
sand from holy places.

And then? Then he came back.

3

She was waiting for him at the dock,
to receive him, face to face.

Her hair – old cobwebs;
the child trapped in her palm.

Her flesh was like a sieve,
she was dressed in lace :

the nights had eaten her alive.
He cried, he wailed;

his tears fell
onto her live wounds.

She cried, of course she cried.
Then they set forth.

4

Those who go on voyages
seldom come back holy.

He wasn't holy when he left.
No wonder he came back.

Still Life

As they sat together, silent
in the blazing sun,
a full moon came and blessed them.

Her fingers dripped love,
his eyes shut in wax.

These lovers!

How they brought upon us
a night exceedingly white
in the noon of day.

No News

There is no one tonight in the courtyards of the moon.
Except for the winter mulberry-branches
and my clinging eyes –
there is no one.

There is no one tonight in the courtyards of the moon.
Except for the mulberry-tangles
and your consuming memory –
there is no one.

Is there a spell for this hour?
Except for the women spinning
and my streaming blood –
there is no sound.

There is no one tonight in the courtyards of the moon.

Last Confession

Eye to eye.
The white moon grinds my light
like millstones.

Forehead to forehead.
The full moon swells on my flesh
like leeches.

Mouth to mouth.
The holy moon swallows my air
like locusts.

Beloved,
for you I dance,
to you my nights are vowed.

I have no other shroud.

The Claim

1

No letters, photographs, dedications.
Now we are in the hands of memory.

I'm glad you didn't give me this autumn,
the moment when sea gives in to moon.

No scratches, love-wounds, bites.
Our flesh says only first rain.

I'm glad I didn't give you that night,
the moment of the muezzin.

On the day of judgment – they will all, all, rush to the bench.
And we will stand there, innocent, without fear.

2   THE WITNESSES

Two sunsets (autumn) on the shores of the Mediterranean,
a pair of horses who came to plunder the evening sands,
a salt wind that watched our tongues,
a fat woman sizzling like a frying-pan, in a deserted café,
chairs stacked up behind us like dossiers –

'They darkened the eyes of the earth
unsheathed a branch from its leaves
destroyed our dream like locusts
blotted out yes they blotted out earth's memory – '

Twilights, two, on the hills of Jerusalem,
children, hidden in the bushes, who threw stones at us,
eternal soldiers (ours) painted on the wall of an emplacement,
a coat of arms hanging on the gate of a hotel,
a lock tensed like a listening ear –

'They didn't talk
they opened the floodgates of silence

brought an end to our flesh
rose yes they rose very high – '

We are ready for the verdict. All the truth, hand and thigh.
But the trial, in fact, is superfluous:
lovers are always guilty from the first
to the last of their limbs.

3 WHO BY FIRE
Fire is a natural symbol of life and passion, though it is the
one element in which nothing can actually live.

SUSANNE K. LANGER

Your honour:
always with torches, with fire familiar and strange,
with parades, with rocketing words,
moaning of sirens, heroics,
desperate ladders to heaven –

always with torches, with masks of the salamander,
echoes of I-am, flare of the phoenix,
split-tongued seraphim,
sparks and voices from heaven –

always with torches, with rain-haloed moons,
tides that smoulder and fan,
broken-lunged runners,
billowing, receding horizons –

Your honour:
always with torches, and at dawn, ash.
But perhaps this once
                            (we confess, have confessed our guilt)
air, and earth, and water.

4

We came down upon the ridge like spring rain.
The surprised colours cried out and the smells burst
    from all sides.
No, we didn't mean to awaken. But the painted soldiers
    on the sides of the emplacement

24

woke up – we stood without cover – fired!
A volley of old eyes –
then they sank back into ambush.
So many years in the rain and wind and oblivion.
No, we didn't mean to stir up. But eyes, an army of eyes,
    bloomed in her hand.
They passed over me in single file. They examined
    all the lines of my hands, asked my back
if it would turn, my face – would it fall.
Eyes, an army of laughing eyes, shut upon me without fear.
The sun set innocently, the children rose.
They threw sad stones at us,
    and shouted in a strange tongue.
We got up and left.
No stone hit us.
No stone could hit us.

5   WHO BY THE SWORD

A sword is above us on Jerusalem's hills
sharp upon our necks
                    and we are double-edged

A sword is above us in the target's grove
drawing out our eyes
                    and we are double-edged

The thrust of the distance and the border's howl
a siege of birds and a treetop's flash

A sword is above us on Jerusalem's hills
biting and raging
                    swallowing our air

But we will stand there naked
(Oh little spies, eyes upside-down!)

We will stand there without breathing
A sword is above us on Jerusalem's hills

But again we will turn over
                    mouth-to-mouth

Your honour:
it was the sea, the sea.
I couldn't comb my hair.
Do not look down upon me because my head is disheveled.

We sat on the beach,
there was a strong wind.

Sir:
it was the sea, the sea.
I can hardly hear.
Please speak up.

We sat on the sand, in the wind,
close together,
and were filled with the whisper of hands,
the thunder of sea-shells.

Your honour:
it was the sea, the sea.
I can't see you.
Do not look down upon me because I'm invisible.

We sat on the beach,
there was a strong wind.
The sea answered, we didn't ask.
The fishermen reeled in their rods.
The sun set.

High priests blessed us.
I was afraid to look her in the face.

7   HER DREAM

I am sailing in a ship of windows.
My eye is glued to the side –
          a dappled gold-fish.
The ship sails on.
A cloud of my breath hides
his house from my eye.
I cannot say a thing.

1964

26

Transition

The eucalyptus shattered the autumn nights.

Oh what a shameless lament!
In the moon's eye
it cracked the silence of windows,
plucked sleep from the birds.
What an abomination
thus to scatter among us
all the shreds of its days!

And now
(what a wailing there was!)
now it stands
on the mound of its silent skins,
ruddy and soft,
in the heart of another season.

Four Air-Letters

I burned your letter.
It's autumn now.
Tatters of bark hang
from the eucalyptus trunk,
like clothes that are out of style.
I piled up its leaves; it flamed,
changed to ashes.
Then I took off my shoes, sat
for seven days and seven nights,
waiting for the little phoenix
to rustle its wings.

Oh I shall brood over these ashes
until my soul takes flight.

A scrap of shoulder,
part of an ear,
an eye like a grape.
All have joined in a sudden
plot to deceive me.
I go on putting you together
like a jigsaw puzzle.
I go on calculating
you and the end of days.

Soon you will be held in my hands,
redeemed,
whole.

3

Now the clocks are changing:
your time is carried on the waves,
skips like a dolphin.
Mine trudges upon heavy earth.

What happens to sundials at night?
What happens to hourglasses
and angel-wings in water?

But when you tell me,
I'll tell you how many grains
of sand, and how many stars,
and how much the time is.

4

I'm sending you many words today,
equipped with light and air and emergency
oxygen masks.

But they have a long way to go,
and who knows
if they've got enough wind.

When they reach you, my love,
you may have to revive them,
mouth to mouth.

Night of Mirrors

At your side – and my dream is on you,
is in you, and at your side. I enter
and your breath says: 'Come,
she is waiting for you like darkness
for the opened eye. You were here,
now you are doubled, tripled.
She waits for you, all, like light for sunrise.
Like a beach for the echoes of the rain.'

At your side – and my dream is of you,
is in you, and at your side. And your breath.

Aquarelle

Silence around me, as water over the sea
Tiny bright-coloured lives
Our mouth filled with water and song

Now I am the wave that lifts you
Now the soft light, the shadow
And the spear

Carefully, carefully we listen
To the transformations within us
To the code of the moon and the shadow

Of the spear.

To the Pomegranate Tree

Go away. Go.
Go to other eyes.
I wrote about you yesterday.

I said green
to your branches bowing in the wind,
and red – red – red –
to your fruit shining like dew.
I called light to your dank
obstinate root.

Now you don't exist.
Now you're blocking the day
and the moon that has not yet risen.

Come, beloved
(I wrote about you two days ago,
and your young memory
stings my hands like nettle),
come look at the strange pomegranate tree:
its blood is in my veins, on my head, on my hands,
and it still is planted in its place!

Condition

First I'll sing. Afterwards, perhaps I'll talk.
I'll return to the words I said

like a man rehearsing his face at dawn.
I'll retrace my silences

as the moon wanes.
I'll swing the cry-bird around and around my head

like a boy drawing his sword at Purim.
I'll court your closed hands

like a lantern growing endlessly black. Yes,
I'll return, I'll be silent, I'll cry,

and I'll sing. First I'll sing. I'll wrap the words
in paper bags, like pomegranates.

And afterwards, perhaps we'll talk.

Transformation

A moth fell on me this morning.
With a flick of a dark wing it erased
all the correct birds,
the smell of coffee, a crying baby (mine),
and in the distance – a whistling train, the rhythm of
    hammers.

Gradually the morning returns to me :
large, exultant, false.
If anyone's face lights up
at me, I will look
for the shadow of the wing in his eyes.

Spectrum

for Moshe Spitzer

1 BLACK

Let us lock the doors
with seven locks and a bolt
let us close the shutters
let us turn off the lights

and let us assume

with a quiet shadowy voice
like someone speaking out of sleep
like water in the heart of a well

let us assume

without mirror
repentance or atonement
once and for all and this one time

let us assume

that these are the last words
which will leave my mouth

2 THE CHAMELEON'S WORDS

My ear was glued to the window-screen
My tongue was inviting flies to dinner

I heard the end that you never spoke
I was shadowy as your darkness

Now I'll redden like a pomegranate
get greener than an almond

I can't help it
There's a rainbow in my blood

Every time I fall
a different colour awakens in me

My dreams are very colourful
I heard the end that you never heard

3   RED

A sea of pomegranates throbs within my eyes
A well of life, a well of life
The moon will dance before me
To bless my nights

A jubilee of sunlight is trumpeting my name
I shall not want, I shall not want
The hours will awaken me
To scarlet praise

The voices of the spring-rain are rising through my days
You're pardoned now, you're pardoned now
For every man is rash, is false
And a sea in his eyes.

Blessing of the Moon

1

The light-years are shut off,
the many waters quenched.

An ancient echo tells me
my blood still flows.

But if I keep on sitting here,
staring,

instantly
I'll turn into a fossil.

2

A child will pick me up,
like a snail,
and say:
Look, you can still see the spirals
of his smile.

A fragile woman, cabbalist of style,
will put me upon her shelf,
among amber beads and a vase
and dewy souvenirs of herself.

She will wait for the oohs and aahs:
So young, and already a fossil!

3

Won't I be able to get up,
to climb out of this well,
to frighten the passers-by
with guesses of moss?

Too late.
Stay where you are.
Your hair has turned white.

Girl in the Closet

What does my coat tell you
when you shut yourself, barefoot, in the closet?
And my big shoes –
two wells of evil shadows?
What do my empty pockets tell you,
and my pants, wrapped around your neck?

I can only guess.
Your muted crying leads an orchestra
of hangers and hooks.
Your face follows the darkness
like a sick sunflower.

I stand in the lighted room and say nothing.
You will have to get out
by your own tears, by your own hands:
the key is in my empty pocket.

Through the Windows

The windows are open,
and light-fish swim secretly into all the rooms.
Now they will nibble at the bait of our eyes,
and the fisherman will calmly laugh.

Flooded by twilight,
we will sink quietly in our rooms,
far from the help of the riverbank
and the fisherman's laughter.

Examination of Conscience
Before Going to Sleep

for Dan Pagis

The driver wasn't even aware
that he'd run over the little bird.
Suddenly it had a name
and address, a colour to its wings.
It lay in the middle of the street,
thrown onto its back,
feet lifted in a diagonal V.
Strange,
even truckdrivers noticed it now,
spread over it
a whistling tunnel. Finally
a pedestrian came
and gave it a last kick.

All this happened in broad daylight,
to the sound of buzzsaws
from a nearby carpenter's shop.
Meanwhile night has come.
I suppose the bird
is still there, clinging
to the gutter's edge.
I note it among the things
I should forget.

The Sacrifice

*Even though Isaac did not die, Scripture honours him as if he
had died and his ashes had been strewn upon the altar.*

MIDRASH HAGADOL

Last night I dreamt that my son did not return.

He came to me and said:
When I was little and you were,
you would not tell me
the story of the binding of Isaac,
to frighten me with knife, fire, and ram.

But now you have heard her voice.
She whispered, didn't even command –
(her hand full of voices and she
said to your forehead, to your eyes:)
is it
so?
And already you ran to the hiding-place,
drew out the knife, fire, and ram
and in a flash
your son, your only one.

Last night I dreamt that my son did not return.
I waited for him to come home from school,
and he was late.
And when I told her,
she put her hand upon me
and I saw all the voices
he had seen.

Somebody Like You

You must hurry in order to hear
what the sleeping child said.

When you arrive
the muted syllables have already sunk
back into his dream.

You must hurry in order to be there
when they lick the shore, come
to rest.

Somebody, somebody like you,
must identify them in the light.

Shockwaves

The air is hurled, is hurling.
I look at your forehead :
widening swirls, circle
chasing circle, chased, growing
in the expanses of your brow,
between your eyelids of day
and your hair at night.

O my mirror, now all is mixed together :
my face, a piece of sky, wisp of cloud, wing, leaf –
widening banks, swirls
of white stone and night stone.
I'm sorry for your forehead.

Meanwhile, there's someone as high as my thigh
and someone as high as my eyes –
learning to look in our mirrors,
to tell the image from its double,
the reflection from its water;
and afterwards they will have to learn
how much one must forget
and how one learns, like us, not to remember,
how not to remember –

But the air is hurling, the air is hurled,
O my mirror, forehead, face –
the soul of you, the body of you !
The soul and the body
are not ours.

Memorial Day, 1969

In Memory of Y. H.

1

She orders vegetables by phone
and arranges, arranges the house.
It's hard to think about her.
There are terrifying screams in her navel
but the line has been disconnected.
It's hard to think about her.
If she is connected –
it's only to the earth:
an ear of flesh and blood to an ear of dust,
and she listens, she listens to the terrifying voices.
It's hard to think about her.

2

He goes to work in the morning,
his chin cries
and his sunglasses laugh.
I met him at noon.
His eulogy was brief:
'It'll be three months tomorrow,
he got an A-minus on his finals.'
I was afraid to look at him as he left:
loaded with dirt and rock,
a porter of memories –
how will he manage to cross the street?
I was afraid to look at his face:
a man without a profile,
without a now –
how can you shake his hand?
He is missing a dimension,
and he doesn't have time.

3

We discussed the margins and the typeface.
I too like precision,
and many dates are written in my notebook.
On other pages are:
a shorthand account of night-birds,
and terrifying voices at noon;
syllables of panic,
and silences, in a first draft.

In Memory of Leah Goldberg

1

A pigeon and a crow
live on the tiles of my house.
A little boy sees them
and says:
God's playing checkers on the roof.

2

A sudden gust of pigeons.
They felt the hurled air before I did.
Now the windows shriek,
and the boom is in my ears.
Leah is dead.
The pigeons are small in the sky.

3

This patch of sky is hers.
She fenced it in
with a few lines, a few stanzas,
and put a bird there.
The little bird flies on patrol
and chases away all the scarecrows.

4

She used to stand at her window for hours:
outside she saw a horse's tail
flicking away the sirocco,
another window shutting its owner,
another window staring like a lake,
a window with a mezuzah
for guests from another season,

a window where a bee crouches
with hair on its belly.
No, she said,
take this bee away.
I am inside, it is outside.
No, she said.

5

She used to sit at her window for hours,
like a collector with a magnifying glass.

6

She had a boyfriend, three years old,
who gave her his hand as she walked down the garden stairs.
As soon as she touched his hand,
the cement split open
and they disappeared among the waves of roses.

7

She loved Chagall,
and wasn't ashamed of that.
She loved,
and was ashamed.
She could refuse to love,
and wasn't ashamed of that either.

I never saw more
than one flower
in her room.

A View of Jerusalem

To Tamara

1

Soft light, green
of treetops – one green,
the fir; another,
the pine. A blue nest in the middle
for the morning bells – one bell
for the fir; another
for the pine.
    That is what the eyes see,
that is what the ears hear
in the northern window. There is nothing,
nothing like Jerusalem,
in which this distance says
something obscure, muted
and explicit.
    The birds see the sound,
my wife sees the birds,
and I cannot lie to her.
There is nothing.

2

Child, child, little flower,
can I already play with you at words?
If I say to you that mine is ours,
that the button opens and none can close,
that the flower closes and none can open –
                    come here beside me.
Even when the sun is shining,
walk in the middle of the street.
When the street-lamp is before us,
put your shadow in mine.

When the street-lamp is behind us,
your hand in mine.
                    Always be visible,
within range of eye and voice,
and I will teach you games of hide-and-seek.

3

Naked. Bone, stone, sky.
Sirens drain our blood,
air foams in the wake of their sound.
Open wide. Dust – blind – and ashes.
Windowpanes make room for eyes,
eyes for the sound of sirens.
That is all a man is, now.
                    Take off your clothes.
I have to touch you.
Now.

4

Everyone speaks in song:
thinks one thing,
and says another;
says one thing,
and thinks.

A winter landscape filled with clocks.
A man puts on his smile like a coat.
Don't look at the lining.

The mine is a name.
The raid is a door.
The trap is a part.
There is no thing
that does not compel its opposite.

A grammar of fears.
The rules – extremely sudden,
and it's hard to talk.

One thing is clear :
everyone plays.
And another thing :
you are no exception.

5

Now. Tomorrow, will surely come,
in my window.
And the walls without a window?
The windows covered with stone?

My wife sees the birds
hidden,
her eyes wide open.
I see my wife :
in the noon of night,
a silver dome at her right hand :
in the dark of day,
at her left a dome of gold.

Sirens in the eyes
and stones from a wall.
(Flash of entangled horns.
A nail glittering in the Roman sun.)
A stone rises
like a small cloud –
                    child, child,

little hand,
can I already say to you Jerusalem,
soft light, tomorrow, another green.

(after the Mahaneh Yehudah explosion, 1969)